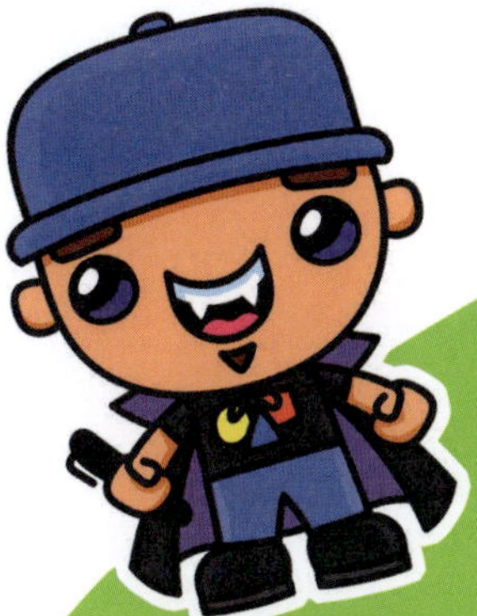

Draw with ART FOR KIDS HUB

HALLOWEEN

30 step-by-step drawing projects inside!

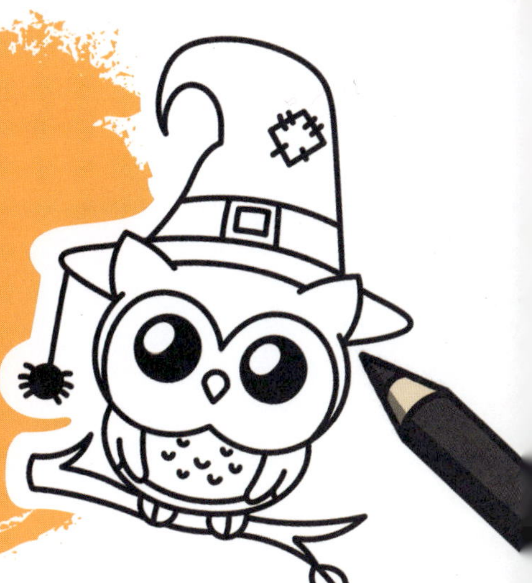

Rob Jensen

Designer Emma Wicks
Senior Production Editor Jennifer Murray
Senior Production Controller Louise Minihane
Senior Acquisitions Editor Pete Jorgensen
Managing Art Editor Jo Connor
Managing Director Mark Searle
Written and Illustrated by Rob Jensen

Designed and Edited by Elizabeth T. Gilbert and Rebecca Razo
at Coffee Cup Creative, LLC.

Copyedited by Beth Adelman

First American Edition, 2025
Published in the United States by DK Publishing
1745 Broadway, 20th Floor, New York, NY 10019

Page design copyright © 2025 Dorling Kindersley Limited
DK, a Division of Penguin Random House LLC
25 26 27 28 10 9 8 7 6 5 4 3 2 1
001–339833–August/2025

© 2025 Art for Kids Hub

All rights reserved.
No part of this publication may be reproduced, stored in or introduced
into a retrieval system, or transmitted, in any form, or by any means
(electronic, mechanical, photocopying, recording, or otherwise), without
the prior written permission of the copyright owner.

No part of this publication may be used or reproduced in any manner for
the purpose of training artificial intelligence technologies or systems. In
accordance with Article 4(3) of the DSM Directive 2019/790, DK expressly
reserves this work from the text and data mining exception.

A catalog record for this book
is available from the Library of Congress.
ISBN 978-0-5938-4390-1

DK books are available at special discounts when purchased
in bulk for sales promotions, premiums, fund-raising, or educational use.
For details, contact: DK Publishing Special Markets,
1745 Broadway, 20th Floor, New York, NY 10019
SpecialSales@dk.com

Printed and bound in China

www.dk.com

www.artforkidshub.com

Draw with ART FOR KIDS HUB
HALLOWEEN

30 step-by-step drawing projects inside!

Rob Jensen

Welcome to Art for Kids Hub!..............6
About This Book.........................7
Art Tools & Supplies....................8
Getting Started........................11
All About Color........................14

PART I: Step-by-Step Projects....16

Bobbie the Bat.........................18
Vinnie the Vampire.....................20
Jack-o'-Lantern........................22
Zeke the Zombie........................24
Burt the Zombie Burger.................26
Wanda the Witch........................28
Mitch the Mummy........................30
Seymour the Monster....................32
Lucky the Black Cat & Pumpkin..........34
Woofy the Puppy Witch..................36
Bubbles the Cauldron...................38
Skully the Skeleton Kitty..............40
Boo-Boo the Spooky Potion..............42
Twila & Flame Spell Book & Candle......44
Spinny the Spider......................46
Kitty Cat Costume......................48
Hazel & Sweep the Hat & Broom..........50
Tombstone of Terror....................52
Richie the Raven.......................54
The Who-Witching Owl...................56
Haunted House..........................58
Sweet Little Scarecrow.................60
Floaty Ghost Buddies...................62
Bones the Dancing Skeleton.............64

Table of CONTENTS

Harvest Moon & Tree Monster............ 66
Dinosaur Costume...................... 68
Poisoned Apple........................ 70
Pumpkin Patch Party................... 72
Cornelia the Candy Corn............... 74
Ghastly the Grim Reaper............... 76

PART II: You're an Artist!....78

Symbols............................... 78
Speech Bubbles........................ 79
Action & Movement..................... 80
Halloween Magic....................... 81
Putting It All Together............... 86
Folding Surprise Drawings............. 88
Folding Frank......................... 90
Cute & Creepy Cupcake................. 93

About the Artist...................... 95
Some Words of Gratitude............... 96

Welcome to Art for Kids Hub!

Hey, friends! I'm Rob. And along with my amazing wife, Teryn, and our four creative kids, Jack, Hadley, Austin, and Olivia, we make art together as a family—and we love sharing it with you! Halloween is such a fun time of year, and one of our favorite ways to celebrate is to make lots of spooky drawings.

This book is divided into two parts. In Part I, you'll find step-by-step drawing lessons for a variety of Halloween-themed projects. Each drawing is ranked Level 1, Level 2, or Level 3 according to its difficulty (see the Symbol Key on the opposite page). Don't worry, though! You'll be able to draw all the projects by following along step by step.

In Part II, you'll find tips for drawing backgrounds, props, and completed scenes. I've also included some silly and spooky folding surprise drawing projects at the very end. Whether you're a beginner or a budding artist, there's something fun for everyone.

Ready to begin? Grab your art tools and some paper, and let's make Halloween art that brings smiles and creates joy!

ROB

TERYN

AUSTIN

JACK

OLIVIA

HADLEY

About This Book

For each project, follow the steps in red to complete your drawing. Then add color using your favorite art tools. It's as simple as that!

1

2

3

Symbol Key

Each project is marked with one of the following symbols, from less difficult to a little more challenging. But don't be afraid to try them all!

 = Level 1

 = Level 2

 = Level 3

 = Great work!

MORE IN THIS BOOK

☑ Draw a magic wand, coffin, candy bucket, and other Halloween-themed props.

☑ Combine drawings to make completed scenes.

☑ Create fun folding surprise drawings.

Art Tools & SUPPLIES

Here are some art tools you can use to draw and color the projects in this book. These are some of my favorite supplies, but you can use any tools that are available to you.

Black Marker

I like to draw with a permanent black marker for a bold, solid outline. But feel free to begin your drawings with pencil if you prefer.

CHECKLIST

- ✓ A flat drawing surface, like a table or clipboard
- ✓ Marker paper
- ✓ Black permanent marker
- ✓ Pencil and sharpener
- ✓ Coloring tools, such as colored pencils, markers, and crayons

Paper

White marker paper is perfect if you're using markers to color, and regular paper is fine if you're using crayons or colored pencils.

Markers

Markers create smooth, solid strokes of color. Some sets include both fine tips and thick tips. I use alcohol-based markers because they dry quickly, and their colors don't fade easily.

Crayons

Wax crayons are inexpensive and easy to find. Sometimes they create a bumpy texture and can be hard to blend, so I use gel crayons. They are creamy and extra smooth.

Colored Pencils

These tools are clean and simple. You can even layer them to blend and shade. Keep a sharpener on hand for pointy tips.

Pastels

There are two types of pastels: soft pastels and oil pastels. Soft pastels feel like chalk and create smooth, light blends. Oil pastels feel more like crayons and create bold, bright strokes.

We would LOVE to see your drawings! Learn how to share them with us here.

Brushes

Brushes come in a range of sizes and shapes. Brushes with natural bristles are best for watercolor paints, and synthetic bristles are best for acrylics. When you've finished painting, rinse your brushes with soap and warm water, and reshape the bristles before they dry.

Paints

Watercolor, tempera, and acrylic are water-based paints that you can use to color your art. Be sure to use them on sturdy paper, such as watercolor paper. While you paint, keep a cup of water nearby for rinsing your brushes—and have plenty of paper towels on hand for cleanup.

WATERCOLOR

TEMPERA

ACRYLIC

Getting STARTED

Before you begin drawing, it's a great idea to warm up. From dots and swirls to dashes and curls, make all sorts of marks on scrap paper to get the creative juices flowing.

I use a lot of loops, dots, and curvy, squiggly, and jagged lines in my drawings. What other lines and scribbles can you make?

Basic Shapes

Most of the drawings in the book start with basic shapes like circles, triangles, squares, and ovals. Practice drawing these basic shapes and then draw new shapes of your own, if you like.

TRIANGLES

CIRCLES, OVALS & BEAN SHAPES

SQUARES, RECTANGLES & DIAMONDS

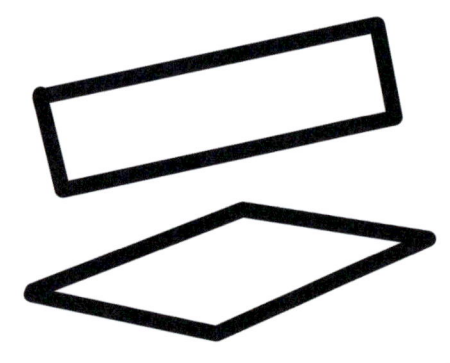

"A happy expression is my favorite, but it's fun to draw other emotions too."

Expressions

The face reveals a character's emotions. In the examples below, see how the eyes, mouth, and other features can help you communicate feelings and personality.

HAPPY	SCARED	SILLY
ANGRY	SNEAKY	TIRED
EMBARRASSED	SWEET	EXCITED

All About COLOR

The Color Wheel

The color wheel is a visual aid for understanding how colors work together. The colors on this wheel are divided into two groups: primary (blue, yellow, red) and secondary (green, orange, purple).

Complementary Colors

Complementary colors are two colors that are opposite each other on the color wheel. When they're placed next to each other in a drawing or painting, they appear brighter. Some examples are yellow and purple, blue and orange, and red and green.

Color Temperature

Colors are divided into two temperatures: cool and warm. Blue, green, and purple are cool colors. Yellow, orange, and red are warm colors. Color temperature plays a part in the mood of a drawing. For example, cool colors are calm and warm colors are energetic.

WARM

COOL

Color Mixing

Every color combination begins with the primary colors. Secondary colors are made by mixing two primary colors. Yellow + red = orange, red + blue = purple, and blue + yellow = green. Gray is made by mixing white and black, while pink is made from a combination of white and red. White lightens colors; black darkens colors.

Coloring Steps

To bring your characters to life, try this three-step approach to adding color.

Add smooth, flat areas of color with your tools of choice.

Layer your colors—or use slightly darker shades—to create shadows.

Finish coloring your art by adding highlights with white.

I like to get creative with color in my drawings! How about you?

Part 1: STEP-BY-STEP PROJECTS

Hey, art friends!

To draw the Halloween-themed projects in this section, start with step 1 and continue to follow each new step in red. Along the way, you'll find lots of encouragement, helpful art tips, and even some fun and interesting facts.

I had so much fun creating these drawing lessons, but we especially love drawing together as a family. So, in addition to my drawings, you'll also see tons of great drawings by Teryn, Jack, Hadley, Austin, and Olivia. Each of us has our own art style, and we want to inspire you to draw in your own unique style, too. There are no mistakes and no wrong ways to make art—the important thing is to have fun and practice!

Happy creating!

Bobbie the BAT

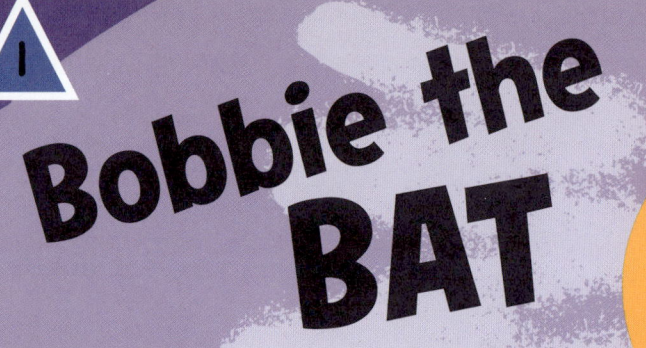

DID YOU KNOW?
Bats are nocturnal, flying mammals that are most active at dusk. With sharp fangs and strong claws—and an eerie upside-down sleeping position—it's no wonder these creatures of the night have become symbols of Halloween!

Follow the steps in red to draw your own bat. Don't forget to share it with us!

You can make your bat creepy or cute! I gave my bat rosy cheeks.

Draw two circles for the eyes and a V for the nose. Then start the head.

1

2

Add the ears and finish the nose.

3

4

Draw the top of the head and the body. Then add the fangs, claws, and top of the wings.

5

6

Use curved lines to complete the wings.

7

3 Vinnie the VAMPIRE

Begin with the eyes and mouth. Then add the head, teeth, and body.

1

2

3

Follow the steps in red to draw the hairline, hands, ears, feet, and other details.

4

5

6

Finish by adding the necktie, cape, and ghosts.

7

8

Jack -O'-LANTERN

Draw the eyes, mouth, teeth, and top bump of the head.

1

2

Add the tongue. Continue drawing the pumpkin; then add the stem.

3

4

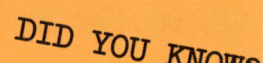

DID YOU KNOW?

Jack-o'-lanterns may have originated in Ireland, where people carved scary faces into turnips and illuminated them to ward off evil spirits.

Finish the pumpkin and add the leaf, vine, and lines around the eyes.

5

6

Draw the eyes and mouth. Begin the head and add a bite mark.

1

2

3

Follow the steps in red to finish the head and begin the body.

4

5

6

Draw the arms and legs.

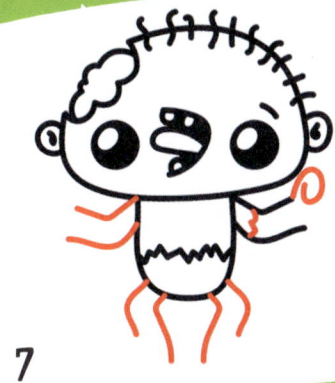
7

8

DID YOU KNOW?

According to folklore and pop culture, zombies are hungry for human brains! Luckily they have a slow (but spooky) walk, giving us all a good chance to escape!

Finish with a bone, finger, and shoes!

9

25

3 Burt the ZOMBIE BURGER

Draw the face and burger top.

1 2 3

Finish the top bun and add some toppings. Draw bags under the eyes.

4 5 6

Follow the steps in red to add details, like sesame seeds and oozing cheese.

7 8 9

Wanda the WITCH

Begin with the eyes, head, and hat rim. Then add hair and a mouth.

1

2

3

Follow the lines in red to draw the hat and body.

4

5

6

Finish the dress, hat, and wavy hair.

7

8

2 Mitch the MUMMY

"My mummy has green skin under its bandages, but yours can be any color you like. I'd run away from this guy!"

Where do mummies go swimming? In the Dead Sea!

Draw the face and head.

1

2

3

Begin adding the bandages, body, and arms and legs.

4

5

6

Continue to follow the steps in red.

7

8

Draw in the rest of the bandages.

9

DID YOU KNOW?

Unlike zombies, mummies are real—but they don't walk around! Mummies are bodies that have been preserved after death. In ancient Egypt, priests wrapped embalmed corpses with linen, inspiring the appearance of the mummy we recognize today.

31

3 Seymour the MONSTER

Adding highlights in the pupils and darker shadows on the underside of each eye helps them look round and shiny!

For extra fun, draw more colorful, crazy creatures from your imagination and throw them a monster's ball!

Begin with the main eye and mouth. Use a gumdrop shape for the body.

1

2

3

Add lots of eyes, teeth, a tongue, and stubby limbs.

4

5

6

Connect the eyes to the head using squiggly lines. Finish the details.

7

Try This!

Draw more monsters with different types of skin. Spotted, slimy, hairy— anything goes in the monster world!

Lucky the BLACK CAT & PUMPKIN

"Use a yellow marker to add a highlight around the eyes to make them pop."

"If you like, you can turn this pumpkin into a jack-o'-lantern instead! Turn back to page 22 to learn how."

Start with the eyes and a V for the nose. Begin the head.

1 2

Finish the face and add the ears. Draw an oval with a stem.

 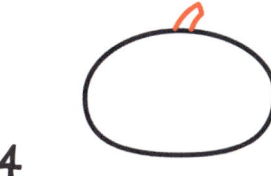

3 4

Continue to follow the steps in red.

5 6

Color your drawing!

Try This!

Cast a spell and turn your pumpkin into another cat. Add ears, whiskers, and a tail.

35

2 Woofy the PUPPY WITCH

Start with the eyes, nose, and mouth. Add the muzzle, brim of the hat, and ears.

1

2

3

Finish the head and add the limbs. Begin drawing the bent hat.

4

5

6

Follow the steps in red to complete the hat, cape, and arm bands.

7

8

36

Bubbles the CAULDRON

Try This!

Try adding other creepy things to your witches' brew. How about snakes, worms, or bugs?

Begin by drawing the face, drips, and edge of the cauldron.

1

2

3

Add a bubbly top, tail, and wings.

4

5

6

Follow the steps in red to complete the drawing. Don't forget the bubbles!

7

8

39

Skully the SKELETON KITTY

Begin by drawing the eyes, nose, and head.

1

2

3

Finish the face, ears, and bow. Draw the body and feet.

4

5

6

Now add the tail, whiskers, and final details.

7

8

40

Draw the opening of the bottle and the ghost coming out.

1

2

3

Draw the bottle. Then draw the potion, ghost, and skull. Begin the cork.

4

5

6

Complete the cork and add bubbles!

7

Try This!

Snakes, centipedes, and spider legs would make creepy additions to a potion! See page 85 to draw a potion brewing station.

43

Twila & Flame SPELL BOOK & CANDLE

Use a rectangle to draw the book.

1

2

Give the book a thick cover and begin its face. Start drawing the dripping candle.

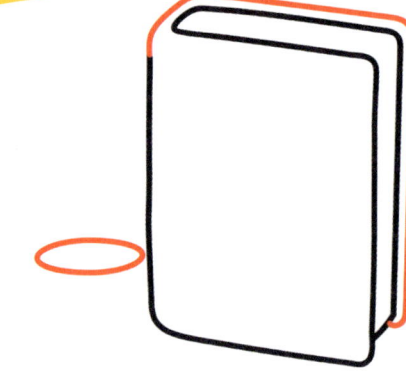

3

4

Follow the steps in red to continue.

5

6

1. Draw the eyes, body, and top of the mouth.

4. Finish the mouth and add eight legs. Draw four straight lines to begin the web.

7. Use both straight and curved lines to build the web.

9. Keep spinning the web until it's done!

DID YOU KNOW?
Spiders are known for having eight legs, but most spider species also have eight eyes! Despite this, spiders generally have poor eyesight.

Kitty Cat COSTUME

Begin by drawing your trick-or-treater's face.

1

2

3

Draw the hair and costume hood, including the kitty's ears and nose.

4

5

6

Complete the hood and draw the body and treat bag.

7

8

9

2 Hazel & Sweep the HAT & BROOM

Start with a gumdrop shape. Add the broom handle, hat buckle, and faces.

1

2

3

Follow the steps in red to create the hat and broom outlines.

4

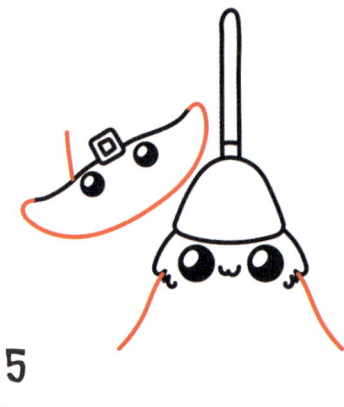
5

6

Finish the details to bring your drawing to life!

7

Tombstone of TERROR

Start by drawing a bit of dirt and an arm bone. Draw a U for the hand and an oval for the grave.

1

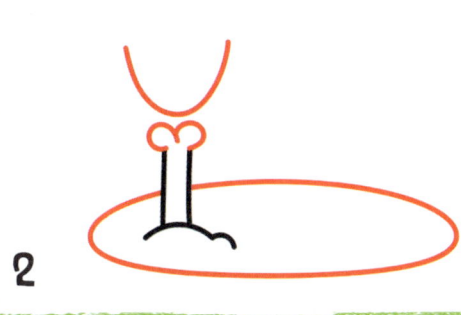
2

Continue to draw the hand. Add more dirt and start the tombstone.

3

4

Add the fingers, rocks, and tombstone details.

5

6

Draw blades of grass and more dirt. Add eyes to the skull.

7

53

Richie the RAVEN

Begin by drawing the eye and head.

1

2

Outline the chest, beak, wing, and legs.

3

4

Follow the steps in red to finish the beak, tail, and feet.

5

2 The Who-Witching OWL

Draw the eyes, head, ears, and nose.

1

2

3

Follow the steps in red to fill in the details.

4

5

6

Finish the hat, branch, and feathers.

7

8

DID YOU KNOW?

A common symbol of Halloween, the owl is a nocturnal bird with a spooky call that sounds like "hoo hoo." Its special feathers allow it to fly quietly in the night, helping it sneak up on unsuspecting prey.

Complete your drawing and then add color!

9

57

Haunted HOUSE

Use simple shapes to build the house from the ground up.

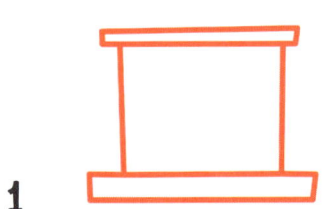

Continue to add the details.

Finish the ghosts, bats, and pumpkins.

Try This!

To make your house even spookier, you can add cobwebs, a black cat silhouette, or even some tombstones in the yard! See pages 81 to 85 to learn how to draw Halloween-themed props.

I drew a bat silhouette against the glowing moon.

I made the roof red and the house brown. The glowing eyes in the door sure look creepy!

Begin by drawing the face, head, and scraggly hair.

1

2

3

Draw the hat, body, suspenders, and straw.

4

5

6

Follow the steps in red to complete your drawing.

7

8

Floaty GHOST BUDDIES

> Draw partial bean shapes for the ghost bodies. Add eyes and the top of the mouth.

1

2

> Follow the steps in red as you draw!

3

4

> Finish the faces. Then add hearts to complete your drawing.

5

3 Bones the DANCING SKELETON

"Your skeleton's bones don't have to connect. In fact, loose bones are better for dancing!"

"I would tell a skeleton joke, but you wouldn't find it very humerus."

Begin by drawing the eyes, skull, and body.

1
2
3

Use short lines to add mouth and rib details. Add arm and leg bones.

4
5
6

Use circles and bones to complete the arms and legs. Begin the hands and feet.

7
8
9

Finish with the fingers and toes.

10
11

65

Draw the monster's eyes and mouth. Then add the tree base.

1

2

3

Give the tree a flamelike silhouette with gnarled branches. Add the moon.

4

5

6

Follow the steps in red to add the moon's face, craters, and other details.

7

8

2
Dinosaur COSTUME

Draw the trick-or-treater's face under a row of dinosaur teeth.

1

2

3

Now draw the dinosaur's head, face, arm, and body.

4

5

6

Finish the limbs. Add claws and a candy bucket.

7

8

9

Start with the apple's stem and leaf.

1

2

3

Draw the dripping poison and the curved bottom of the apple.

4

5

6

Finish with one more drip.

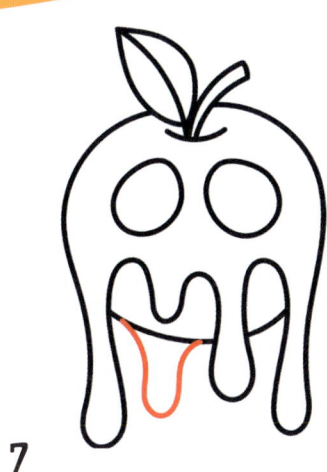
7

Try This!

Switch up the colors for fun! Use red for the dripping poison and green for the apple's skin. Try adding eyeballs, too.

2
Pumpkin PATCH PARTY

Use rounded shapes to create a group of pumpkins. Add a couple of stems and a leaf.

1

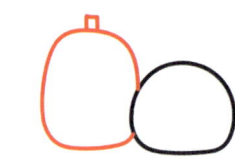
2

3

Continue adding to the pumpkin patch, giving each one a pair of eyes. Draw the wooden sign.

4

5

6

Finish by adding the signpost, faces, and more leaves.

7

8

Cornelia the CANDY CORN

Draw the mouth, eyes, and top of the candy corn.

1

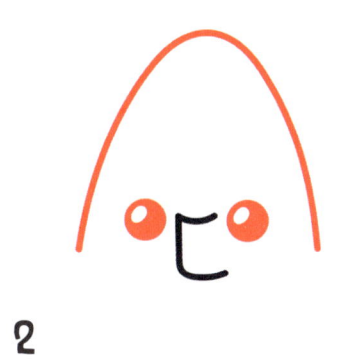
2

Complete the candy corn shape. Add teeth, eyebrows, and a tongue.

3

4

Draw the limbs. I added light lines in step 6 to show you where to add color. You don't have to draw those lines unless you want to.

5

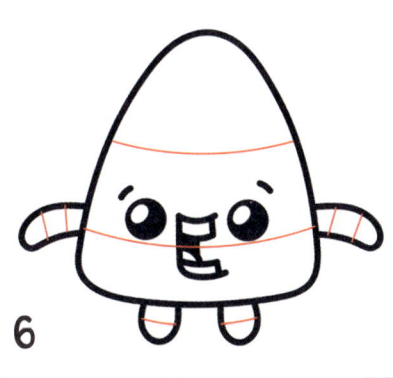
6

That's good enough to eat!

Try This!

Give your candy corn a hat, shoes, or its own Halloween costume if you'd like.

Ghastly the GRIM REAPER

2

Begin by drawing the eyes, nose, and a row of bumpy teeth. Then start the skull.

1

2

3

Use curved lines to draw the swirling hood.

4

5

6

Follow the steps in red to add the body.

7

8

9

Part II: YOU'RE AN ARTIST!

In this section, you'll learn how to draw things that add interest to your art. I've also included instructions for creating two folding surprise drawings. Remember, there are no mistakes—your only goal is to have fun!

Symbols

Symbols can be used to express emotions, feelings, or a state of mind. For example, replacing a character's eyes with hearts suggests they might be thinking about love. Drawing sparkles around a potion gives it a magical feel. What other symbols could you add to your drawings?

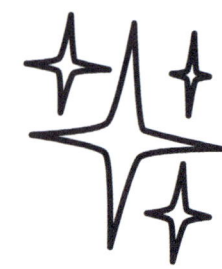

SPARKLES
Use sparkles to show something magical.

HEARTS
Hearts are great for showing affection and emphasizing cute things.

STARS & LINES
Stars and lines can help suggest motion, such as the woosh of a witch flying on a broomstick.

Speech Bubbles

Add personality to your characters with speech bubbles that show what they're saying or thinking.

Round and rectangular speech bubbles give your characters the ability to "talk" to each other or your readers.

This speech bubble is used to express enthusiasm or excitement!

This thought cloud reveals a character's internal thoughts to the reader.

What Austin said.

Action & Movement

These fun details can add interest to your Halloween drawings by showing them in action and bringing them to life.

CRACKLING
Use curved lines with little bursts at the tips to show the popping of embers from the fire.

GROWLING
Squiggly lines can suggest anger, trembling, or even noises, like a monster's growl.

SWOOPING
Use long, curved lines to show the downward swoop of bat.

BUBBLING
Use a group of little circles in different sizes for bubbles, and add a few bursts to show them popping.

FLOATING
Draw a fluffy cloud so your characters can float— and add some bursts for a magical touch.

FLYING
Wavy lines show how the owl is flapping its wings and flying through the air.

Halloween MAGIC

Props are objects that add character, style, and a sense of place to your drawings. Turn the page to see some more cool things you can draw and combine to create magical works of art.

Powerful Potions

Begin by drawing the corks. Then add the bottles, making each one a different shape. Add some creepy contents and some bubbles!

Halloween is such a fun night! I love thinking of things that would make a scene even spookier or more festive. In addition to the props on pages 81 to 85, how about drawing some fun costumes—like a bee, a spider, or a fairy?

Magic Wand

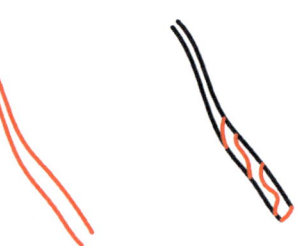  

Draw the crooked stick and wood grain. Then add the handle and a burst of light.

Flying Eye

 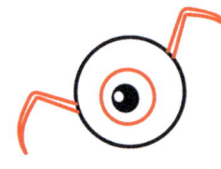 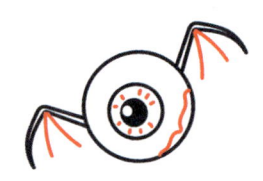  

Draw an eyeball with an iris, leaving a white highlight. Add batlike wings and a tail. Follow the steps to complete the drawing.

Melting Candle

Draw the top of the candle and the wick. Then add drips, the sides of the candle, and the flame.

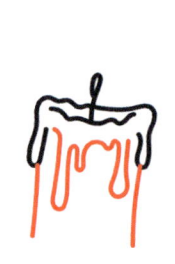  

Cauldron

Draw a scoop for the pot. Then add the lip, logs, and flames. Don't forget the bubbling brew!

Begin by drawing the glass jar. Add the floating brain and lid with a handle. Finish with a few bubbles.

Brain in a Jar

Lantern

Use rectangles and straight lines to draw the lantern. Finish with a handle, flame, and lines to emphasize its glow.

Candy Bucket

Draw the jack-o'-lantern bucket. Add the handle, and fill up the bucket with candy!

Spider & Web

Start with the corner of a square; then follow the steps in red to fill out the web. Don't forget the spider!

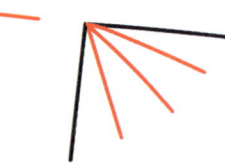 

Coffin

 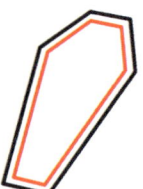 

Use a geometric shape to draw the coffin. Decorate it with a skull, and add latches to keep it sealed shut.

Tombstone

   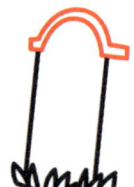

Start with the base of the stone and the grass. Follow the steps in red to complete your drawing.

Broken Clock

Draw the clock's case and face. Follow the steps in red to add cracked glass and some fancy details.

String of Lights

Start with a curved line. Add tiny parallel lines in pairs for the light holders; then draw circles for the pumpkins and complete the faces.

Candelabra

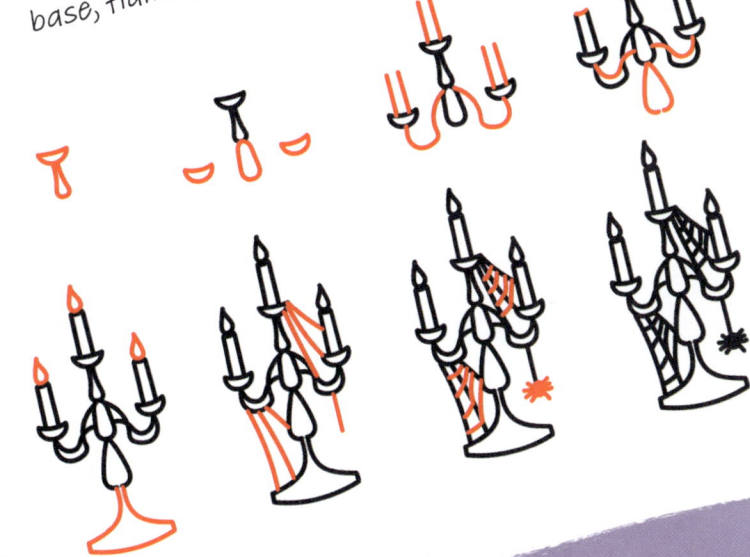

Draw the metal holder and candlesticks. Add the base, flames, cobwebs, and a dangling spider.

Brewing Station

Draw the table with a bent leg. Add the potion bottles and a trunk. Finish the details.

85

Putting It ALL TOGETHER

Look how you can pull all the individual pieces together to form completed scenes. What other scenes would you like to draw?

Witch's Den

Folding SURPRISE DRAWINGS

A folding surprise drawing is exactly what it sounds like: a drawing on folded paper that opens to reveal a surprise inside! This project is a lot of fun and gives you an opportunity to stretch your creativity.

Before you begin, you'll need to prepare your paper so the surprise works the way it should. I used a sheet of printer paper (8.5" x 11"), but you can use any size paper you like.

Paper Set Up

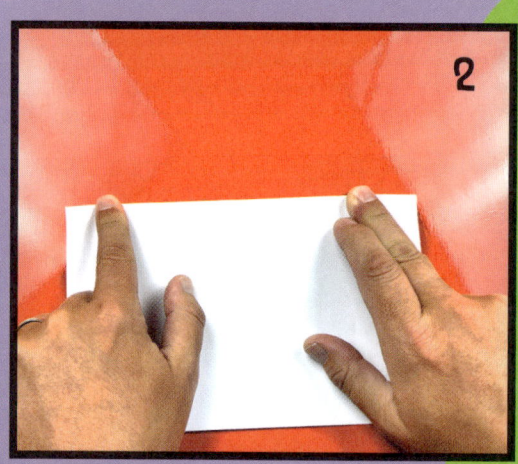

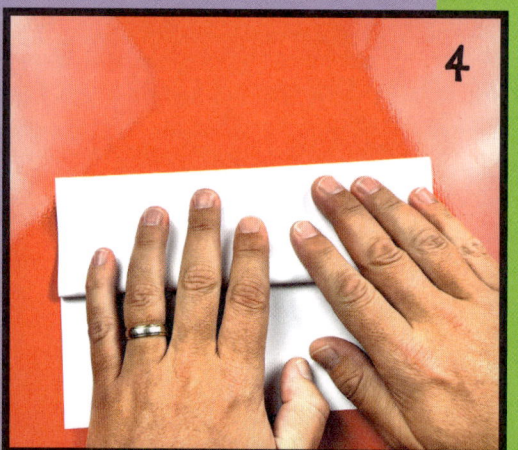

1. Lay the paper flat with the short sides of the paper on the top and bottom, and the long sides of the paper on the left and right. Fold the paper in half, lining up the top edge with the bottom edge.

2. Press along the fold to make a crease.

3. Gently lift the top flap of the paper.

4. Fold the top flap up, bringing the bottom edge to line up with the top edge. Press along the fold to make another crease.

5. and 6. Lift the paper and flip it over from right to left, so that the unfolded bottom flap is now on the top.

7. Lift the flap and fold it up to meet the top edge, repeating step 4.

8. Open the last fold you just made.

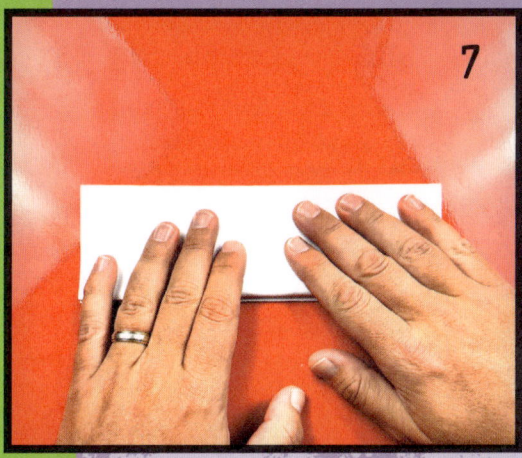

9. Flip your paper over from left to right, so it's back to the original side.

10. Your paper is now ready for your drawing! You will start the outside drawing on the folded paper.

Note: When you unfold the page, you should have four sections marked by folds.

Turn the page to get started on the first surprise drawing!

2
FOLDING FRANK

FOLDED

1. Place the paper with the folded side up (see step 10 on page 89). Draw a cup shape for his head.

2. Use short, vertical lines in a row to create Frank's stitches. Draw these lines along the fold line. Add two circles for eyes and a wide nose under the fold line.

3. Connect the sides of the head to create a block-shaped face. Then add pupils and two half circles for ears.

4. Draw a zigzag line to show his hairline. Follow the marks in red to add the mouth and a few more face details.

5. Finish by adding nostrils, two rounded teeth, and a bolt on each side of his neck.

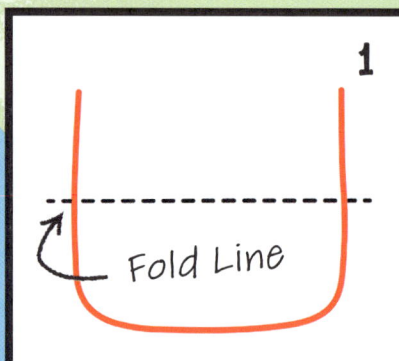
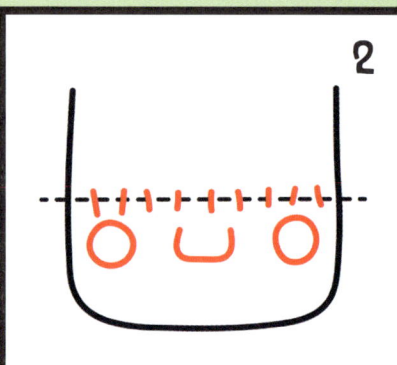
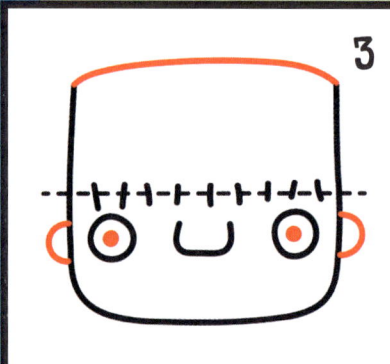

Turn the page to see how I colored Frank.

OPENED

1. Draw a cloud shape between the top and bottom fold lines.

2. To begin the brain's face, add two circles for the eyes and a C shape for the mouth.

3. Add pupils and the tongue. Draw zigzag lines above and below the brain to represent electricity.

4. Connect the first two zigzag lines with two more zigzag lines. Finish the mouth.

COLOR YOUR DRAWING

1

1. Refold the paper so only the outside drawing is visible. Then add color with the art tools of your choice.

2

2. Open the paper. Now color the insides of Frank's head! I used pink for the brain, red for the tongue, and a combination of yellow and orange for the electrical burst.

92

3 Cute & Creepy CUPCAKE

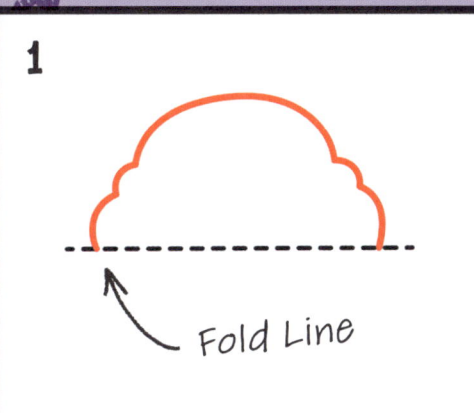

FOLDED

1. Place the paper with the folded side up (see step 10 on page 89). Draw the top of the fluffy frosting with curved lines.

2. Draw two circles for eyes, leaving a white highlight in each. Then add the bottom of the frosting just under the fold line.

3. Draw a mouth, eyelashes, and a birthday hat on top. Then draw the base of the cupcake.

4. Add sprinkles and frills next to the birthday hat. Draw vertical lines on the base of the cupcake.

Don't forget to color in your drawing. For added fun, give your cupcake monster some birthday candles!

OPENED

1. Unfold your paper so the cupcake is split. Draw frosting lines below the top fold and above the bottom fold.

2. Now add super-sharp teeth extending from both frosting lines.

3. Draw a curly, split tongue coming up from the cupcake bottom.

4. Add the sides of the frosting behind the tongue using small, scooped lines.

5. Draw more party hats, the sides of the mouth, and some claws.

6. Follow the lines in red to add sprinkles and the final details.

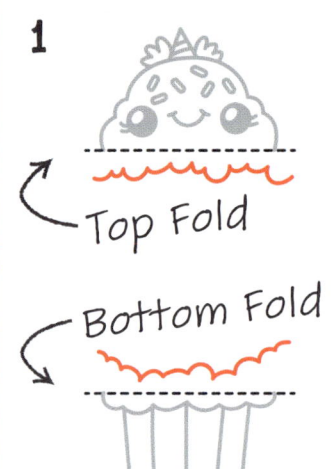
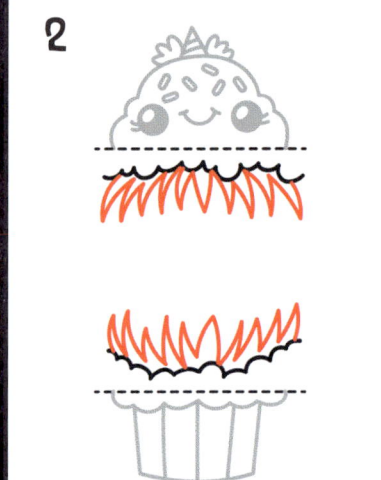

ABOUT THE ARTIST

Rob Jensen, the fun-loving creator of Art for Kids Hub, has a background in industrial design, which fuels his passion for teaching art. He believes that creativity adds happiness and interest to life. Rob, along with his family, embodies the spirit of making art both easy and exciting. Collectively, the Jensens demonstrate that art is not just a solo journey but a shared family adventure. Together, they show the world how to create art in simple, engaging ways, one drawing at a time.

ABOUT ART FOR KIDS HUB

Art for Kids Hub is a family-driven platform that brings the joy of art to families around the world. Co-created by Rob Jensen and his family, it offers a friendly, welcoming space for kids of all ages to learn and grow artistically. Recognized by various media outlets, Art for Kids Hub provides a diverse range of resources, including an engaging website, an online shop, and social media content full of art lessons. This platform is committed to making learning art fun and accessible, showcasing that art can be a delightful experience for everyone. It complements traditional art teaching by adding its unique, family-oriented touch. Visit artforkidshub.com.

SOME WORDS OF GRATITUDE

In the creation of this book, I've been surrounded by an incredible circle of support and inspiration, each person contributing uniquely to this journey.

To Teryn, my wife and partner in everything: Your love, support, and friendship are the cornerstones of not only this book but of all our endeavors. I am endlessly grateful for your presence in my life. You make everything possible.

My deepest gratitude also goes to our children—Jack, Hadley, Austin, and Olivia. Your creativity, laughter, and shared joy in art have been the foundation of not only this book but all we do at Art for Kids Hub. You are my heart and inspiration.

A heartfelt thank you to DK, my publisher, for believing in this project. Pete Jorgensen, who first reached out to me with this wonderful opportunity: Your confidence in my work has been a great honor. Working with DK has been an enriching and fulfilling experience.

Special appreciation goes to Rebecca Razo and Elizabeth Gilbert at Coffee Cup Creative, LLC. Your expertise and vision have been instrumental in bringing this book to life. Your dedication and skill have transformed my ideas into something tangible and beautiful.

To my parents, Greg and Ruth Jensen, thank you for your unwavering encouragement and support since my childhood. Your belief in my passion for drawing has been a guiding light throughout my life and career.

I am also profoundly grateful to the young artists and their families who have joined us on Art for Kids Hub. Your enthusiasm and creativity have been a continuous source of inspiration and joy.

To the broader community of educators, fellow artists, and supporters, thank you for your encouragement and invaluable feedback. You have helped foster a nurturing space for young artists to thrive.

This book is a tribute to all of you. Your support, in so many ways, has made this journey an enriching and joyous adventure. Thank you for being part of our art family!

Rob Jensen